T0065579

"Absolutely"

An Intriguing Story

William Emdee

authorHOUSE®

AuthorHouse™
1663 Liberty Drive
Bloomington, IN 47403
www.authorhouse.com
Phone: 1 (800) 839-8640

Published by AuthorHouse   08/18/2016

ISBN: 978-1-5246-2501-6 (sc)
ISBN: 978-1-5246-2500-9 (e)

Print information available on the last page.

About the Author

I am from Upstate New York. I am retired and like to spend my winters in Florida. I took up writing about six years ago, and I am working on my third book. I do hope that you will find this book intriguing.

This is one hell of a story that I am going to, tell you. If you don't believe any of this, I don't blame you readers at all. It's all fiction anyway…

Everything I am about to tell you started back in 2000. My brother Terrance (Terry for short – that's what I call him) and myself, William (everybody calls me Bill which is the short version of William), stumbled upon something really weird! I think it was a Saturday sometime in early May. It was pretty chilly out that day. Terry and I were riding our dirt bikes in the hills around Belcourt, part of the Black Hills of Dakota, it was in the afternoon and a nice day, no snow was on the ground so riding our bikes was going to be cool. We had been riding for probably 1 ½ hours and decided to take a break. We stopped on this slight rise and could see a long distance off to the south. We had never been out there before. Deciding which direction we wanted to go, we both had our energy drinks, so we laid our bikes down and sat on the rear wheels and looked out over the country side. Like I said, towards the south you could see a long distance.

Off to the west, we noticed a gulley which went into some low hills. I said to Terry that we should explore that area and he agreed. We both like riding and exploring different geographical areas. Finishing our drinks, we started up our bikes and off we went into the small gulley. Riding slow and carefully we rode on. As we came upon this jutting wall of what seemed like concrete which was typical dirt, gravel of this area, Terry's bike sputtered. We stopped and he tried to clear it up by revving it several times. It seemed to clear up and we continued on. We went around this wall and advanced further up the gulley and I mean up – slight, but up – probably 200 feet, we were probably half way up then Terry's bike just quit – I mean died there going up that hill. I stopped and waited for him to start up again. Nothing happened, no matter what he tried, that bike said no. He had gas, but no spark, she was dead. Well, now what do we do, miles from wherever, 2 guys one bike? Terry left his bike where it died, couldn't lean it on anything, couldn't stand it up, so he left it lying on the ground. So, now we were climbing up hill and I had to really push my bike to go up. When we stopped we lost momentum and to start up hill with a dirt bike one can run into difficulties with balance and traction – don't need for either of us to get hurt, so we walked and pushed. At the top of this rise we stopped and looked around to get our bearings. We could see nothing but gullies, talk about being screwed up – we sat down to analyze our situation. Both of us agreed it wasn't good, this wasn't our first encounter with difficult situations, we had been in tough spots before. But, here we were out in the middle of nowhere, Two of us on one bike that typically holds only one. We did have our backpacks and they were packed with the things needed for tough times. We had on our riding clothes which was good for what we were doing, but if we had to stay very long out here, they might not be good enough. When things like this happen, water and food are your main concern. Terry said "boy we are up that proverbial creek without a Paddle".

Let me tell you a little about Terry, he is what you would call a confident, rugged, capable, reliable, wonderful person. Terry is 27 and he and I were born on the same day, only two years apart, him being older. How Mom & Dad pulled that off no one knows. Terry has a BA in accounting and works for a firm in Rapid City – me on the other hand, no college for me. I went into the Marines right out of High School and did two tours in Iraq, now living in upstate New York. I came west for 2 weeks' vacation and spent time with my parents and Terry. Terry is a bachelor living the good life, good job, good money and doing pretty much what he wants. Now he is stuck with me out in the middle of nowhere. It's getting late and the sun is setting low and getting chilly. We decided to sit tight until morning and then see what we could do about getting out of there. Survival is imperative when you're lost – we had food stuff and water bottles enough for a few days if we were careful – couldn't build a fire to keep warm, no wood out here. So, to keep warm we decided to dig a depression in the ground next to a small wall that had a flat surface on it. That way we both could lay in it next to each other and use our backpacks for some cover and that way we could survive the night. Temperatures at that time of year drop pretty low at night. Terry and I had a small drink of water from our bottles and some energy bars from our backpacks and we sat and talked while we ate. We both are survivalists – more than once we have been caught out in places where we couldn't make it home in one day, so this set back doesn't concern us. Dark descended on us so we crawled into our hole and covered up best we could, not too bad for comfort, but come morning it might be colder than we will like!

We made it through the night. The temperature didn't drop as much as we had thought it would. Still pretty chilly – we both had another energy bar and some water and decided to move out of there, it was daylight now and the sun was just breaking over the horizon. I picked up my bike and started pushing it to the top of the rise and Terry had his backpack on and I thought he was behind me. I looked back and he was on his knees with something in his hands looking at it. He hollered at me to come back, so I laid the bike down, dropped my backpack next to the bike and walked back down to where Terry was. He held in his hand a rag, well, what looked like a rag. As I came up to him I could see he held what was a piece of deer skin. He said that when we were digging our hole to sleep in we must have dug it up. He carefully unrolled this deer skin and inside was two round objects. Both were about 6" long and 1 ½" around and, at the top was a hole about 1" down, and a leather cord was strung through them, like to hang around your neck. It was some kind of bone, deer or elk. Each one was like the other, there were 3 sets of double lines horizontally, and two lines vertically in each set of those lines, talk about weird. We looked them over really carefully and had no idea what they were, guessing some Indian about to die, didn't want anyone to find them on him so maybe he buried them – who knows. Anyway, we had dug them up and now we had to find out what they were. I said to Terry it was a good find but gold would have been better – He laughed at that, Terry always had a good sense of humor, not much bothers him. I thought, at the time, maybe those two items were Indian Magic Sticks but we would take them to someone with knowledge about the local Indians and see what they say. Terry rolled them back up into the deerskin and stuck them into his backpack. We needed to get out of this situation we were in. So, back up the hill we went. I pickup my bike and looked around, Terry came up beside me and said "where the fakawi"? That old saying came from the Fakawi Indians – they were always lost and the chief kept saying "where the fakawi"? Anyway, we could see pretty far being up on this knoll, we could see to the end of the hills that we were riding in. I said to Terry we somehow had to mark this rise so he could go back and get his bike. The only thing to use was his survival knife and his handkerchief, so Terry plunged his knife into the dirt, and tied his handkerchief on to it. Then we headed on out of the hills, pushing my bike. About an hour later we reached asphalt. I let Terry take my bike and go and go and get his pickup. I would sit and wait. He returned and we recovered his bike that day and went to his house and collapsed.

Terry had to get back to work so he left the objects we found with me and I started researching Indian artifacts on the computer. I spent all day and didn't see anything like our objects. The next day I looked up people who dug up things, a college was a good start. I found out the University at North Dakota has an Anthropology department, a telephone number was also listed, so I called and a lady answered the phone. I told her what I had and would like to talk to someone with knowledge about Indians and artifacts. She patched me through to a Ms. Joan Beck who was an Anthropologist, knowledgeable in such things. OK, that will work. I talked to Ms. Beck and told her what we found and she was very interested in seeing them. I made an appointment for Saturday at 11:00 AM, that way Terry could be there, as he doesn't work weekends. Terry's apartment is in Devil's Lake about 2 hours northwest of the University of North Dakota. We arrived on time at the university, and went to the building we were told where to go to and went inside. We didn't see anything that resembled the department we were looking for, so I stopped a young person carrying a load of books and asked for the Anthropology department. We were told that Ms. Beck's office was on the second floor, so up we went. We found Ms. Beck's office and went in. Ms. Beck was waiting and she ushered us into her office. We introduced ourselves and shook hands with her. Looking at her I thought wow, what a beautiful woman. Terry took over immediately and I kind of stepped back so Terry could do his thing. By that I mean that Terry must have had the same response to her as I did. Terry doesn't spend a whole lot of time with women. He's devoted to his job and that doesn't leave a whole lot of time for other things. I have to give him credit for the way he lives, kind of frugal yet he has his toys. He has told me he wants to pay back his education loan as quickly as possible, so spending money on dates is not something he does often. Well, anyway, Terry took out the deer hide, with the two objects inside, and laid it on a large table in Ms. Beck's office. I was anxious as to the reaction Ms. Beck would have when she saw both objects. Terry untied the bundle explaining how we came upon the things. He rolled the deer hide out and stepped back. I watched her face as she looked at the 2 objects. She just stood there and looked. After a few minutes, I said "go ahead and pick them up". She said "please wait a minute" and went over to the phone and placed a call to someone we didn't know. She hung up and came back to us and offered us coffee. We both declined. Ms. Beck said "you men have found some very unusual objects and I want our head of the department to see these". About that time the door opened and in came an older man I'd say about 80, not so fast but agile. Ms. Beck introduced him as a Professor Dunham. We shook hands and explained what we had and how we got them. Professor Dunham picked up one object and held it in his open hand looking at it. Terry asked him what he thought they were. Professor Dunham didn't say a word, he just stood there looking. Then without any word, he laid the object back down on the table and turned around and went over to a bookshelf where there were dozens of books kept. Terry and I just looked at one another and gestured with our mouth not saying anything. I said to Ms. Beck "is something happening here?" and she said to please wait until Professor Dunham finished his observation of these two objects. I looked at Terry and raised my eyebrows. Professor Dunham finally selected a book and came back to the table. He opened it up and went through the pages until he came to one particular page he wanted. He then explained that in this book he has before us it might show something that was similar to our objects. He then showed us the page he had chosen and right there in front of us was a picture of the same objects we found. So Terry said "so these objects aren't that important"? Professor Dunham said "whoa-whoa-whoa, hold on young fella, what you have found is extremely important". The one in the picture is the only one known to modern archaeology. This particular object was found in Mexico back in the 30's!! Now located at Cornell University in New York. Professor Dunham said to us "boys would you be willing to leave these with me for further research?

I would like to confer with others in my field". They will be safe with me. I will say this "these two objects are extremely rare and I will guard them with my life"! Ms. Beck said she had never seen anything quite like these objects before and said that they might be Aztec from Mexico, but how would they make it all the way to North Dakota, as old as they seemed to be? That was another thing Professor Dunham wanted to do was carbon date them and see how old they were. When I was in Iraq I did see lots of artifacts and was impressed with the importance of the past. So, I looked at Terry and said "I wouldn't mind leaving them if he didn't". He agreed and I did ask Professor Dunham for a receipt signed by him and he agreed. Terry, in the meantime, was googling Ms. Beck. I think something was starting up with my brother, I have never seen him act this way with a woman. Professor Dunham gave me the receipt for both objects and thanked us for bringing in this important find and shook our hands and said he would be in contact through Ms. Beck. I think Terry liked that idea better than finding those two objects. We left Professor Dunham's office and went into Ms. Beck's office. We gave her our names, address and cell phone numbers, that way she could contact either of us. I kind of figured she might call Terry the way he was fumbling around. She gave both of us her business card and Terry's eyes lit right up – now he had a phone number. She said she would be in contact with us in the next few days. We thanked her, shook hands, Terry longer than me, and we left for home. It was close to one o'clock and my stomach was talking to me. I asked Terry if he wanted to get some lunch before heading home, he said "definitely, I'm starving" so I drove downtown. We found a nice looking restaurant, went in, and found a booth. A very pretty lady, maybe in her early 20's, came to take our order. She introduced herself as Lucy and asked for our order. I introduced us and she asked if we were new in town? Yes, I said we had some business at the university. She said "that's where I go to school". I kind of took over the conversation and asked her what it was she was studying? Her answer was "archaeology". Terry and I looked at each other and smiled. Lucy picked up on that immediately and said "what was so funny"? I told her we had just come from Professor Dunham's office, she said that Dunham was her professor and was studying under him. We laughed ourselves silly. Lucy wanted to know what we were doing at Professor Dunham's office and I said just something we wanted to know about an object we found, no definite explanation. I figured we should keep our find to ourselves. Lucy took our order and returned with coffee for us and sat down next to Terry across from me. I looked into her green eyes and I was gone. With red hair and green eyes, this was a very pretty woman. We carried on a conversation until our food was ready. I found out that she was in her 3rd year of college and was going for a Bachelor's Degree in Anthropology. She was working in the restaurant for extra spending money. She told us that she was from Ohio, farm country, and a farm girl, that she hadn't been home for a year and she missed her Dad terribly. Terry told her about him and where he lived and worked. I then told her I was from Upstate New York and that I was a diesel mechanic in a dealership back home – I had learned my trade in the Marine's motor pool while in Iraq. Terry said we would return after we received a call from Professor Dunham sometime next week. The bell rang from the kitchen and Lucy jumped up saying "I will get your food now, be right back". Lucy returned shortly with our order and left us to eat. I said to Terry "wow, did you ever see such a pretty woman as that?" and he said "yes, Ms. Beck". Well, here we were sitting in a restaurant eating lunch in a strange town and already we had met 2 beautiful women. Terry had his eye on Ms. Beck and I had my eyes on Lucy. Maybe those two objects we found had a magical power to them. Maybe good luck charms! Terry laughed when I said that. We finished our lunch and Lucy brought our check. Terry took it and headed for the cash register. Lucy hung back 'til he was away from us and I looked into the beautiful green eyes and then asked her for her phone number. Lucy produced a piece of paper and handed it to me. I opened it up and her phone number was written on it. She had beaten me to it. I looked up into those beautiful green eyes and smiled. I said I would be calling and she replied "I will be waiting"!

Terry and I left the restaurant, jumped into his pickup truck and headed for his place. The following week Terry went to work and I spent my time with Mom & Dad, who live in Devil's Lake, fixing odds & ends that Dad couldn't or wouldn't fix, and just plain visiting. Mom couldn't do enough for me and cooking, you'd think I never ate food before, and my Mom can cook. Dad retired from the telephone company here in 2010 and now he likes his beer and golf. Occasionally, they will go on trips with AARP, bus trips. Dad's not too keen on driving, his eyesight is failing and he doesn't want to take any chances at possibly hurting someone because of him. I love my Mom and Dad and don't want anything to happen to them. They were disappointed when I enlisted in the Marines. They wanted me to go to college like Terry and get an education. I had a hard time getting out of high school so I knew college was out when I was struggling to finish my senior year. I am not dumb, I just don't study well. I am happy with my life and know I found Lucy. Maybe something will develop with Lucy.

I haven't called her yet, really I was waiting for a call from Ms. Beck. It was Saturday again and Terry called around 9:00 AM and said Ms. Beck had called on Thursday and wanted to see us on Saturday at 1:00 PM. I said "come and pick me up already". He said he would be over in about an hour and that we had plenty of time to get to the university. I said "aren't you anxious to see Ms. Beck"? He laughed and said "see you". I told Mom & Dad about the girls we met at the university and you can imagine their reaction. They have always pushed us guys into relationships, hoping someday to be Grandparents. Well, maybe the day is coming, things are starting to look up. Today I will see Green Eyes if she's working at the restaurant.

Terry got to Mom & Dad's around 11:00 AM and talked for awhile, both parents wanted to know why we were going to the university. And, to keep them in the dark, I said I was looking into classes to do online from home. They bought it. I don't like lying to Mom and Dad, but until we know what we found, we need to keep it to ourselves. Terry and I had lunch with Mom and Dad and then took off for the university. We got there around 12:45 PM and made our way up to Professor Dunham's office. We walked in to the office and did we get a surprise, Professor Dunham and Ms. Beck were there, and also Lucy. Professor Dunham said Lucy was there because he had invited her to the inquiry, meaning to help solve the mystery of the two objects I guess. Professor Dunham introduced her to us and we smiled and said we had already met last Saturday at the restaurant downtown. He smiled and said "good, Lucy is tops in his class and he wanted her help along with Ms. Beck's on this project". I don't know about Terry, but I thought that was one hell of a good idea. Terry and I shook hands all around and of course we smiled at the girls a little extra. The professor saw that there was a little more there than just simple hellos. We then went into Professor Dunham's office where the objects were laid out on the table. He then said the girls would explain what has happened since last Saturday and went over to his desk and sat on the corner, one foot on the floor and the other swinging in the air. Ms. Beck, Lucy, Terry and I gathered around the table and Ms. Beck looked at Terry and said "please call me Joan". At that point Terry's eyes lit up and he smiled big time. She said we don't stand on formalities here in the department. Professor Dunham spoke up and said everyone could call him "professor". Ms. Beck, and Joan said the research on the objects was a slow go, meaning they were not making much headway in finding info. Joan said the other object that we had seen in the book Professor Dunham showed us last week was at Cornell University in New York. Somehow it had ended up there. She then said that Lucy had called Cornell University and talked to the department head and asked about the object listed in their book on rare artifacts. Cornell's response was yes the listed object was cataloged into their department and was available for viewing. Lucy said she made no mention of our objects. Joan also said no other research could be found from any text books, so far. Professor said that he thought going to Cornell would be to our advantage, we could compare our objects with the one at Cornell. In the meantime, while everyone was gone traipsing all over the U.S., he would start looking into Aztek artifacts from Mexico. Perhaps the

University of Mexico at Mexico City would know of the objects. He said he had taken pictures of them, so he didn't need to take them to Mexico, pictures were fine, "you folks take them with you, but be careful with them, again, I will say that they are extremely rare and valuable". Now, he said "I want Joan and Lucy to go to Cornell next week and you two boys to chaperone them. The department will pay all expenses, we have funds for this sort of thing". Terry and I both looked at each other and before we made any commitments we needed to talk this over with each other. I said "could I call you on Monday and let you know if we could make the trip back to New York"? Professor Dunham said "no problem, we will wait for your call". We asked the girls to walk us out of the building because we wanted to talk to them. Professor Dunham said to the girls "go". He is a cool guy, sharp but also kind. On the way out I got close to Lucy and Terry got close to Joan. As we walked, we talked. I said to Lucy I hadn't called her last week because of Mom and Dad. I had to explain about their obsession for grandchildren and I wasn't ready to discuss that possibility yet. If I called from the house either one of them would start asking questions so I waited till I saw you today. Terry said he would have to take some sick leave in order to go to New York, but he was going. My vacation was about up so I said we would all fly together. Joan said she would make all the flight arrangements and get our tickets and call us boys when she had everything. I said "tell Professor Dunham that we were going". So, that way we can get things going instead of waiting till next week. Terry asked the girls if they wanted to go to dinner later, no place fancy because we were not dressed for fancy places, but somewhere nice that the girls agree on, and they both accepted. I said "how a about 5:00 o'clock?" and they said that was fine.

Terry had the objects with him and we said goodbye to the girls and we would meet them at a certain place at 5:00 PM. We left the university and went downtown and found a bar. Terry very carefully hid the two objects under the seat in his truck and we went into the bar and ordered ourselves a beer. I said to Terry "this could be a life changing trip you know. Both of us have found girls we really like and we will be together for the next 3 or 4 days. What do you think, Terry"? He said he was looking forward to sitting with Joan on the plane. We can get to know each other really good in 5 hours of flying. I said the same thing for me. I told Terry that I was very interested in Lucy and he said he was the same with Joan. We had found two ladies that we both liked and felt that something might develop further over the next week. While I was sipping my beer, I had thoughts of grandeur. I was thinking about Terry's truck. It is a single seater and wondered how 4 of us would fit in the cab. Terry driving, Joan next to him, me next toJoan and Lucy on my lap. That would be nice. I told Terry what I was thinking and he let out a loud, hilarious laugh and said "Bill, that's a good one. That would be nice for you. Maybe we'll go in one of the girl's cars." I said "it was a good idea". He laughed again. We had a couple of beers apiece and discussed the trip coming up. When it was time Terry and I headed back up to the university to pick up the girls. They were waiting for us where we were to meet them. Terry stopped the truck and I rolled down my window and said "do you girls want to go in your car or ride in the truck"? Both of them said together "we will ride with you guys in the truck". Now things were really getting interesting. I looked at Terry and winked. I opened my door and slid out. Taking Joan's hand I helped her into the truck. Then, I got back in and reached for Lucy's hand. She got in over my legs and I shut the door and Lucy sat down on my lap. I was in heaven. Lucy's perfume and soap scent drifted up into my nose. It smelled like a flower garden. I thought, man, I will get 4 or 5 more days of this. Terry drove back downtown and Joan directed him to this lovely restaurant, but men don't say lovely, they say cool, great or OK restaurant. It was nice. We had our dinner and had a very nice time talking and getting to know the girls. We were in the restaurant perhaps 3 hours or so. It was getting late and Terry and I had a long ride home. We dropped the girls off at the university parking lot and made sure each one drove off before we left for home. Monday Joan called Terry and said we fly out of Grand Rapids on Wednesday morning and we could pick them up in time to make the airport and flight to Ithaca, NY. That is where Cornell University is. Terry said OK, we will be there. I did what little Dad wanted me to do when I told him I was going home on Wednesday. Mom was happy that Terry and I had found two lovely girls and said to bring them home soon. I told Mom "ya, soon",that I really like Lucy a lot and I told her that her oldest son was also fascinated with this beautiful lady he met in Grand Rapids. Mom was thrilled that her two bachelor boys were finally getting their act together. I know what she was thinking "grandkids". What is it about being a grandparent? Dad even mentioned it awhile back about us boys finding someone and settling down. Well, they might get their wish if everything goes OK these next few days. Terry and I picked up the girls at Joan's place and we were off to the airport. We caught our plane on time with Terry and Joan together and Lucy and I back 2 or 3 rows behind them. I think the girls planned this. Anyway, we were on our way to New York. Terry had the two objects in his carry-on and they were in the overhead compartment. Lucy and

I sat back and held hands during the flight. We talked about a lot of things, her family, her growing up, what she was working for, who she would be working for, what she wanted for the future. I told her about myself and everything I wanted – time really flew by and before we knew it we were landing at Ithaca Airport. We rented a car and I let Terry drive to town where we found a nice hotel in downtown Ithaca. We checked in, the girls in one room, Terry and I in another down the hall. We told the girls would pick them up at seven for dinner, that way Terry and I could take a nap because we had been up since 4:00 AM. Both girls smiled and said "OK, see you at seven". Terry and I retired to our room and sacked out for a few hours. We met the girls at seven and went downtown for dinner. After asking several people on the street where the best place to eat was, we found a nice restaurant and had a very nice dinner and a happy time talking. Joan said we had an appointment at Cornell with a Professor White in the morning at 10:00 AM. He was Cornell's top authority on antiques, especially Indian artifacts. This Professor White was part Indian. Joan said he was Seneca, a New York Indian. We finished dinner and walked around town for a while and then went back to the hotel and retired to our rooms. Thursday morning all four of us drove up to Cornell University, its way up on top of hills in Ithaca. Why a university built up here I will never know. It is a beautiful university and big. We located the Anthropology Department and went in to see Professor White. They were expecting us because Joan had called last week. We met with Professor White and his assistant, Mike Brown. Brown and White, crazy! Professor White is one of the few Indian history and Archaeology Professors around and is well known in his circle of Anthropology. We shook hands and made introductions all around and who was what. Professor White was rubbing his hands together and was a bit nervous when he said "please present the two objects you have brought". Apparently, Joan had described them to Professor White and he had some idea at to what they might be. Terry took the roll of Deer hide out of his carry-on and laid it on the table. Then, he untied the roll and rolled out the Deer hide so the Professor and his assistant could see the two objects. Professor White stood there and just looked at the two objects. Then, after a minute or so, he picked one up very carefully, looking it over, turned it around, looked inside, felt the texture of the bone and gently laid it back down. He said to us "Gentlemen, do you have any idea what these objects are"? Of course we didn't or we wouldn't be here, but Terry said "no we didn't ". Terry is the polite one in our family. Well, Professor White very quietly started to explain what they were. He said that these two objects were, in fact, Medieval man or Shaman's Tools of Trade. In other words, he used them when performing ceremonies or curing the sick. But, these two objects and the one's we have here are identical. He said to us that these two objects were a very important find and he was very happy to have them here with the other one. He also asked Terry and I if we could leave them for the day and we agreed, again, asking for a signed receipt! Professor White said he would be available again on Friday morning at 10:00 AM. We said that would be fine. At that time he would give his evaluation and explain everything he knew about these objects. We thanked him, shook hands and left his office. All four of us were outside the building when we stopped to talk. Now the girls had a better idea of what Professor White knew about our objects than either Terry or I, but weren't saying much. So, I said to Joan "let us in on the secret your archaeologist thinks these objects are"! Joan said "you

17

boys just wait until Friday morning and Professor White will tell us everything. We don't have all the information he has and he will explain it much better than us". Terry said "come on, let's get something for lunch" and we piled into the car and headed downtown. After lunch we decided to do a tour of the wine trail north of town. We spent the rest of the day tasting wines of the Finger Lakes. Friday morning we went back up the hill to Cornell and met with Professor White and Mr. Brown – you know, "Brown and White". The people at Cornell must get a lot of mileage out of saying that funny connection. Anyway, we were in Professor White's office and the two objects were lying on a table there in front of us. Professor White started by saying that the two objects were Shaman medicine sticks and that during a ceremony he would hold both sticks at the same time and dance around the fire in a circle. (Indians always danced in a circle because, if they dance in a straight line, now think about it, they would dance straight out of the camp and there wouldn't be anyone left but the chiefs and no one left to fight the Indian wars.) Holding both sticks with the strings of leather around his wrist, he would do his chants, bringing good medicine to the fighting warriors, and in other instances, heal the sick ones. Whether or not they worked, we will never know but the Indians believed in the medicine man. Professor White had carbon dated both objects and said they were from the 15th century and in excellent condition. Why they were where we found them was a mystery to him. The objects are definitely Pueblo, tribes that lived in Arizona, New Mexico area. I told him we found them in North Dakota. He said that someone probably found them or stole them and they took them as souvenirs, but lost them in North Dakota, whoever they were. Being that they were buried, perhaps that person was being pursued and didn't want to be caught with the two objects. Apparently they didn't want anyone else to have them either. He or they would come back later for them but never did. As far as I am concerned, I think they are good luck sticks. Think about it, I came home for a visit, spent time with Terry riding our bikes, spent time with Mom and Dad, we met two beautiful women, took a trip back home to New York, visited several Professors, went to two Universities and I have had a really good time, so far. So, I think they are lucky sticks. Whatever they are, so far they have been good for all concerned. Why Cornell only had one stick no one knows, if a Shaman used two sticks in his business, where was Cornell's other one? After talking with Professor White for a half hour or so, the big question came up, what were Terry and I going to do with these sticks? He said they were extremely rare and very valuable. I looked at Terry and he said that him and I would have to give it some thought. He thanked us and asked for our phone number for further contact. I asked him if Cornell was interested in them and at what price? Professor White said that Cornell was definitely interested in purchasing them for their collection of Indian artifacts, he couldn't offer any monetary figure until he met again with the university higher-ups. We, again said, we would think on it and let him know our decision. Little did I know that Joan had thoughts of her own about the two sticks. We all shook hands with Professor White and Mr. Brown, picked up our sticks and departed Cornell. We went downtown and found a different restaurant. All four of us had lunch and then we discussed everything that had taken place this morning at Cornell. That was when Joan said "the University of North Dakota would very much like to buy the two objects". I said to her "how do you know that?" and Joan said "I have been given authorization to make an offer in case Cornell was interested, and if you two guys were going to sell the two sticks the University of North Dakota has given me permission to offer $25,000 for both of the sticks". Well, that shocked the hell out of me and I looked over at Terry and he was smiling like a Cheshire cat. I said to Terry "I like the price, how about you"? He said he was okay with it, so I said to Joan "it's a deal, you now own both sticks" and all four of us shook hands and then we hugged one another. We finished our lunch and went back to the hotel, packed up our gear and headed for the airport. Before we left the hotel, I gave Joan both objects and said "as long as you own these, you can carry them" and we both laughed, but Joan was very careful as to where she packed them, so that nothing would happen to either object. We caught our plane back to Grand Rapids. I only wished I had time to show Lucy my place there in New York, but some day maybe. We flew into Grand Rapids. Terry and I dropped the girls off at Joan's house and headed for our parents place. We told the girls we would call them sometime next week. Terry said to me on the way to Mom & Dad's place, "I really think Joan is cool and I am going to call her and start dating her". I told him the same thing about Lucy. I said to Terry "I guess it's time for the bachelor brothers to settle down". I said "Mom and Dad will be happy". I told Terry that the last 3 days with Lucy were great and that Lucy was a terrific gal, and I was in love and going to marry her, of course, with her consent. When we got to Mom and Dad's place, Mom had dinner ready, which was very thoughtful. I guess she didn't want her two boys to starve to death. We had dinner and over coffee Terry and I explained what took place over the last 3 days. Terry told Mom and Dad that we had found some artifacts in the desert while riding our bikes the week before and that we went to New

York to Cornell University to see the same thing that they had, and that Cornell wanted to buy them. I told the folks that Joan, on behalf of the University of North Dakota, had authorization to buy our objects, and she offered us $25,000 for them. Dad said "did you take the offer"? I smiled and said "yes". Dad said "I don't know what you had, but that was a hell of a find". Terry and I had discussed our monetary inheritance and what we would do with the money before coming home. I had said "let's send Mom and Dad to Hawaii for a month". He laughed and said that was a good one, and said "ok, let's do it for them". So, while we were having our conversation over coffee, I said "Mom and Dad, how would you two like to go to Hawaii for a month"? Terry and I will pay for everything. I thought Mom and Dad would have a stroke right there. After a while when there was no response, I said "well"? Mom jumped up and hugged me until I thought she would break my neck, and Dad grabbed Terry in a fatherly choke hold and Mom started dancing up and down with my neck! They were so excited and Mom kept saying "yes, yes, yes". I said "ok Mom, we get the idea, you will go, you will go, you will go"! Now let go of my neck. She said "oh, sorry son". Dad was shaking our hands and hugging me also. One big happy family, which for me made me feel good. The first time in my life I could give my parents something. I am sure Terry was feeling the same. Terry said he had to head for home because he had things to do. We stood at the door after he said his goodbyes to Mom and Dad and shook hands and hugged each other and he said "finding those two objects was the best thing that could happen to us", and I said "things are looking up". To other people that saying probably doesn't mean anything, but to my brother it does and he said "you bet". I said call me when you talk to Joan and have the money and I'll get Mom and Dad off to Hawaii. He smiled and said "you bet".

Terry left for home and I returned to the kitchen where Mom and Dad were talking, all excited about Hawaii. They, of course, had to ask about what Terry and I did with the two girls for 3 days. I explained to them that 2 days we were flying and 1 day at Cornell, so not much happened with the two girls. However, I did tell them that Terry and I did really like both girls and we would be seeing them again. I didn't want to get my parents hopes up about Daughter-In-Laws and Grandchildren. It was getting late and I was tired so I said good night to my parents and went to my room. I took a shower and shaved and jumped into bed, then I called Lucy. We talked for an hour and I told her my vacation time was up and I had to return home on Sunday, but I would keep in touch and that I was really happy that I could spend the last 3 days with her, and under the circumstance we had a good time with each other, and I would be back. She said she also had a good time and enjoyed my company and would like to see me again. We said goodnight to each other and I shut off the cell phone. I laid there a while thinking about Lucy and what could develop between us. The next morning I made my reservations to fly home because I still had a job to go to. I called Terry and said I would wait to hear from him. I said "goodbye". He also needed to get back to work on Monday, he said. The flight home was uneventful and I landed at Corning Elmira Regional Airport and went to pick up my luggage. Then I picked up my truck at the long-term parking lot and headed home up I-86 to Bath. Now, Bath, NY may not be a large city, but I like living there. I have a good job and I have a nice apartment and possibly Lucy will think of this place as home also. We'll see. Terry and Mom and Dad have never been here. Maybe I can get Mom and Dad to come for a visit, of course, I will pay for their trip now that I have money. I have money, but this new money I can use for my parents. On Wednesday Terry called and said he had 3 checks, one for him in the amount of $11,000, a check for me for $11,000, and a check for $3,000 for Mom and Dad. He said he would send me mine and Mom and Dad's and to get their tickets and the rest for spending money, which I had agreed with him so that they would have some spending money. I said I would take care of everything and asked if he had talked to Joan any since I left him. He replied "yes, I had a very pleasant conversation with her on Monday night and have a date with her on Saturday, maybe drive to Fargo for the weekend". I said "sounds good". I haven't called Lucy yet, been resting up from the trip, too much excitement I guess. I hung up from Terry and call Mom and Dad and ask them when they would like to head out for Hawaii? I guess they had already discussed their plans and Mom said anytime, the sooner the better. I said I would get their tickets and have them delivered with their travel schedule and hotel right on Waikiki Beach. Mom screamed and laughed and said "Waikiki". She never in her life dreamed of going to Hawaii. Terry sent the 2 money checks and I went to a travel agency in Elmira and made travel arrangements for Mom and Dad. I got tickets for a return flight from Grand Rapids to Honolulu and hotel right on the beach. The rest of the money I put in traveler's checks and I sent everything home to Mom. I put my money into the bank in Bath for now. I don't really need to spend any of it yet. I will save it for a rainy day. I called Mom and said everything was in the mail and for her and Dad to have a great time in Hawaii. She thanked me again and said "I love you". I told her the same. I finally called Lucy and told her what was going on here with work and getting my parents off to Hawaii.

She knew about me getting my money and was happy for me. I said to her how would you like to come back to New York again? I have a nice place and maybe you would like it here. It's about a 1 ½ hour drive from where we were a couple of weeks ago. It really is beautiful country and I am sure you would enjoy it. She said yes. She would like to come and visit me, but not until school is out maybe on spring break. It wasn't what I wanted to hear but schooling is important and I said "I understand". Lucy had told me she was in her third year when we flew to New York and summers were taken up on Archaeology digs. She had said they were working a site in Minnestota, something about an Indian village that was significant to history. We talked for a long while and then ended it. I said I would call soon. I have always had a desire to learn how to fly a small plane and I thought, I have money now, why not learn to fly and buy myself a small plane. On the weekend I drove down to Corning where I have seen airplanes taking off and landing, not really giving any thought that an airport was there. I know there are planes at Corning Elmira Regional Airport but this is a small airport west of Corning where I saw the planes. I located the road to the airport and drove down it to where the planes were. I got out of my truck and was looking around for someone to talk to, then I went over to a small Piper Cub airplane and started checking it out. It was a nice plane, but I wouldn't know a nice plane from a bad plane right now. However, I plan to change that. I was looking around the plane and didn't notice this older man come up to the plane and watch me. After about 5 minutes he said "hello, can I help you"? I jump about 2 feet off the ground at that point. I'm skittish when surprised like that, after Iraq. I told him I was thinking about learning to fly and asked him about it. He said "come on over to the office and

I will tell you how to start". I look at this Piper Cub plane and ask him how much does a plane like this cost? He said somewhere around $50,000 dollars. I almost swallowed the gum I was chewing. Planes cost that much I asked him and he said "some less, some more". I said "do you have to own a plane to fly one" and he said "no, you can rent planes on an hourly basis after you get a pilot license." I thought that was better. I have a good chunk of change in the bank but I couldn't see spending $50,000 on a plane. Maybe it is like buying a used car, prices may be different. Anyway, I walked into his office and took a seat in a chair in front of his desk. He said that he was an Instructor here at the airport and he could teach me to fly. He introduced himself to me as Walter Gunn and I told him my name. we shook hands and he asked me if I wanted coffee. I said "no" and sat back in the chair. Walter gave me all the information about flying a plane and how long it took to get a pilot's license and then he told me the cost. I didn't have any idea that this was going to cost so much. Then he took me out to one of the planes he uses to teach flying and showed me around the plane and what he had to do before flying it. Then Walter asked me if I wanted to go for a ride and I said "I would love to". I had been in big planes but never in a little one, so Walter said get into this plane right here, we will take this one up for a ride, so I did. Walter got into the other side which he said was the pilot's seat. He started up the engine and slowly moved down to the main runway. After about 10 minutes, we reached the end of the main runway and him telling me to hang on because we were taking off. Walter opened the throttle up and the engines roared and down the runway we went. About half way down the runway the plane slowly lifted up and we were flying. It was a good feeling to be up in the air. We flew for about ½ an hour and

Walter said we should go back. I agreed with him. After we turned around, Walter said "would you like to fly the plane"? I said "yes". He explained what to do and I took over the controls and was flying the plane by myself. You need to understand that a plane has the controls on both the left & right side of the plane, anyway, this one did. So here I was flying by myself. The feeling was great. We were flying about 2 thousand feet up and could see everything from there. We flew back to the airport and Walter landed the plane himself. After he parked the plane we went back into his office where he asked me if I still wanted to be a pilot. I said I did and that's when I started working to get my pilot's license. Walter was a good Instructor, tough, but good. He wouldn't let you get by with any mistakes, but like he said once, if the plane's engine quits up in the air, there is no place to park it except the ground and the results are not so good. I did get my license after a while and a nice little Piper Cub came up for sale for a price I could afford. Not too long after that, being that I am a mechanic, word got around the airport a mechanic was around, and other pilots began asking me to check out things that didn't sound good to them. They paid me well. There are probably about 50 or so planes here at the airport and when other pilots heard about me they wanted work done on their planes. It got to the point where I was working on planes and not flying them. Walter came by one day as I was checking out this plane that someone asked me to look at, and he said "Bill, you do so much work around here for these guys who own their planes that it was mentioned that perhaps you would consider working on their planes full time". Walter said I could have a hanger to work in and that there is plenty of work to make a living just keeping all of those guys planes in the air. I said "I would consider his offer". I had a good job at a dealership in Bath and it would be hard to give it up. However, I would be working for myself and could go flying whenever I liked and the money was good. The plane owners had no one who looked after their planes like I did and I would have no out of pocket expense working there, a free hanger to work in and I already had my tool boxes full of tools, maybe I would have to pay something for lights and heat, and telephone, but no large overhead, probably Insurance to cover my butt. I told Walter that I would accept his offer.

Here again, luck was on my side, whether the sticks had anything to do with it, or not, I don't know. That night I called Terry and told him what I was going to do and he congratulated me and said it was a good decision and he asked me about me and Lucy. I told him we were talking a lot and that nothing would happen until she graduated and had her degree. In the meantime, I quit my job at the dealership in Bath and moved my tool boxes to the airport. It took me about a week to settle in to my hanger workshop. I hung signs around buildings and the office indicating I was there at the airport and ready for business. It wasn't long before I had enough work to keep me busy. Lucy asked me if I was going to fly over to see her now that I was a pilot. I told her that to fly that far in my plane would be too expensive, and I would stick to the big planes.

May came around pretty quick and Lucy finished her third year at ND. We made plans for her to fly to New York for a visit. They gave her a week off, and then she had to fly back to Minnesota to work on this dig she had worked on every opportunity she had. I sent her a ticket for New York and I was so happy to see her. It had been awhile since we had been together. We spent a very nice week together. I showed her New York in my area and we went all over sightseeing. I also surprised her with a plane ride one day. I took her to a town west of Corning, about 1 ½ hours away. We went to a nice restaurant and then flew home. Lucy really enjoyed herself. To me she was a lovely lady and someone I could live with the rest of my life. Someone Mom and Dad would love also. And, of course, possible Grandkids. At the end of the week I bought Lucy's ticket to Minnesota. She had brought her work clothes with her, so she was ready to dig right in when she got there. That is what Archaeologists do, dig. I told her that and she thought I was funny and laughed at my remark. Lucy has a good sense of humor and what I liked most about her was that she was sincere, and was a very likeable, beautiful woman. The night before she left, I took her to a nice restaurant in Elmira, not to far from home, and wined and dined her as they say. After dinner I brought out this little box and opened it, took out this diamond ring I had purchased the week before Lucy came and, not being a romantic, I just said "Lucy, will you marry me"? I got the response I was hoping for, she said "yes", but that we would have to wait until she got her degree next year. I said I could wait. I asked her if she felt that she could live here in Bath or Corning and she said she would like living in New York, it was so much different than North Dakota. Of course, her work would take her all over the world. I said I could live with that. I would miss her while she was gone but, I would be ok with that. Lucy went to Minnesota and I went to work planning our lives as I saw it. I called Terry and told him about Lucy and me. He congratulated me and said Lucy was a really great gal and that he hoped we have a good, long life together. I then called Mom and told her. She was so happy that, at last, one of her boys was moving in the right direction, as far as she was concerned. Mothers, they have this desire to be Grandmothers, must be human nature. Anyway, Mom was tickled pink, as she put it, that I asked Lucy to marry me. I told Mom that sometime in the near future I would try to bring Lucy home for a visit, and to meet her. I would let her know when. Dad said he was happy that I was working for myself and to be careful flying those planes.

I decided that if I was going to work on planes, I should know more about them, so I found, online, a school that taught an airplane mechanic's course. It was located in Williamsport, PA, about 1 hour flying time or 2 hours driving time, so I called and made an appointment to see their Instructor. I drove down to Williamsport and found the school. It was a nice looking building, it had a landing strip and there were several planes outside. I met with Tom Wilson, the Instructor, and a pleasant sort of guy. I told him that I was a mechanic and I had my own plane and my own repair shop in Corning, but felt that I need more instructions on small plane maintenance. He congratulated me for me having my own plane and working on planes and the desire to learn more about planes and repairs. He said "a good mechanic repairing and maintaining small planes was worth his weight in gold". So many of the smaller planes are flying in unsafe conditions because of lack of qualified repairmen. People own and fly their planes but rely on good mechanics to keep them up in the air. There are more planes than mechanics. Tom showed me around the shop. They had 3 Instructors plus Tom and about 10 men in the class, so Tom had time to show me around. He explained what the course was about and that it took about 4 weeks to complete. I told him

I was ready to start as soon as I could because I had plenty of planes at home that needed me. Tom said the next class would start the 1st of the month which was about 7 days away. I said that was good and I would be there. We shook hands and I left and drove home to Corning. The mechanical course was expensive but I could afford it. Besides, I had money coming in from my shop. I would have to schedule my repairs for the weekends and do classes during the week, but I felt that I could better serve my customers if I had better knowledge of their planes. So, I started scheduling my workload for the weekends, and plane owners I was working for understood what I was doing and they realized that I could service their planes better with what I learned at school. Any repairs needed while I was at school would wait until I returned. I called my brother in North Dakota and told him I needed an Accountant. He asked me what I was up to so I explained what I was doing. He said he was happy that I went to work for myself and that I was going to school to improve my skills. I then asked Terry if he would do my business and personal taxes. Of course, I knew he would and he said, yes, he would take care of my books and do my taxes. All I had to do was save all receipts for expenses and send them to him once a month. I asked him how Joan was and he said that they were doing well and that he was going to propose to her come Christmas… boy that made me happy, Joan is a very sweet person, plus she and Lucy are friends. So, two brothers marry friends, that's nice, that's good. I told Terry I had bought a small plane and that I could fly home faster than driving, but yet it was still a long ways. I said I had gotten my pilot's license, and the other good news I told him was that I popped the question to Lucy, and that we will be getting married after her last year in school, sometime in May. Then

I said "maybe we could have a double wedding"? He said "that would be a great idea, and that he would run it by Joan and let the girls discuss it among themselves to see if they would like to have a double wedding". "Do Mom and Dad know that you asked Joan to marry?" and he said he had told them he was going to propose, of course Mom and Dad were happy for him. Another prospect for Grandchildren. I tell you, Mom especially can't wait until the little ones start coming around. I don't what it is about being a Grandparent, but Mom definitely can't wait! I wouldn't doubt that she already has a closet full of baby things that she has bought, both blue and pink just in case, see, that way she has covered both bases. In this case it's babies. Laugh, I tell you "Mom is a beaut". Anyway, Terry was happy that he was going to propose to Joan. Terry said that Joan and Professor Dunham had done more research on the two sticks we had found and when we all get together again she will give us a report on everything they found out. I said that Christmas time is a good time to get together because I want Mom and Dad to meet Lucy, so I will let them know I will be home for Christmas and maybe we could all get together at home. Terry agreed. I said "make plans and I will talk to you later, and hurry up".

I started school. There were seven of us in the class which makes it better for everyone and we get more hands on instruction. We had some very good Instructors. They were aware of the fact that I was a Diesel Mechanic, therefore knew I knew a lot more than the basics of engine repairs. Also, that I had my own business and was repairing airplanes. However, there are tricks to every trade and these Instructors taught us those tricks, things I didn't know about airplanes. Cars and diesel trucks I could teach them, but airplanes, I was there to learn everything I could about them. Time went fast and I completed the repair course with flying colors, got that did you, flying colors, airplanes, flying, ok enough of the nonsense. I returned to Corning and my working full time again. My workload wasn't too bad because of my weekends working here at the shop, but I did have several large repair jobs to get started on. With winter coming on, people don't seem to fly as much. Many of the plane owners store their planes inside hangers, but if it is nice weather out, one or two owners will take off and fly for a while. My work load lightens in the winter and I have more time to work on my plane. I set up a corner of my hanger for a lounge or hangout. I built a 10 foot by 10 foot room, put a stove in for heat and chairs and coffee machine. I like my coffee and it's there for anyone who comes in. Also, I installed a satellite TV service so I could keep an eye on the weather whenever I needed. Weather plays an important part in the flying circles. One doesn't just jump into his plane and take off in a storm, like you can in a car. Good way to die. So, I have people hanging around most of the time whether or not I am working on a plane. When it really gets cold I won't be working on any planes until spring because I couldn't afford to heat my hanger – repair shop. Usually here in Corning things begin to get cold after Thanksgiving and my work on the planes will come to a halt.

I revisited my work place in Bath and asked about part time work. They were happy that I came in. Their diesel workload was more than their Mechanic could handle and they were falling behind in work. One of the owners of the dealership had a plane at my airstrip in Corning and I wasn't aware of it until I happened to see him one day at work. He called me over and congratulated me for working here and at the airport and told me which plane was his. I didn't recognize the plane he described but I acted as though I did. He said that come spring when I returned to my shop, that he had work on his plane to do and would discuss with me at that time what needed to be fixed.

Things looked good. Christmas came up and I took a long weekend off from work and flew home to Mom and Dad's and to see my gal Lucy. Terry had made plans to bring Joan home and I went and got Lucy. Mom and Dad were very excited and happy to meet the girls after hearing so much about them. We had a very nice Christmas dinner and the girls helped mom, not only fixing dinner, but to clean up after, which shows they are great girls, not slackers. When things settled down and all cleaned up we went into the den. Mom had coffee and dessert for us in there. That's when we opened our presents that were under the tree. I had bought Mom and Dad something and Terry did also. I bought Lucy a nice necklace. To her it was beautiful, but to me, a man, it was nice. Terry had bought Joan's engagement ring and right there among the wrappings he fell down on his knees and held out the ring and asked Joan to marry him, right in front of everyone, which was cute. Knowing my brother he also was grandstanding. Anyway, Joan said yes and they hugged and kissed. Mom was up and hugging both of them and congratulating them, then it was Lucy's and my turn to get hugged and mugged by Mom. She was so excited and happy that her two future daughters-in-law were there in the room together on this beautiful Christmas day. Of course, Mom had to ask when were we planning to get married? Terry said it was up to the girls to decide if they would want a double wedding. Well, Lucy said she was for a double wedding if Joan was, and, sure enough, Joan agreed. Well, there it was, a double wedding now the question was when? Lucy said not until she graduated and had her degree in her hand, so it was suggested the marriages take place in June, and they agreed and picked June 1st. What a Christmas this was.

Joan and Lucy and Terry and me sat down quietly in a room at Mom and Dad's house and Joan started explaining what her and Professor Dunham had discovered about the two sticks. They were Mayan medicine symbols, something a priest or medicine man would use in a religious ceremony, however the two sticks were not common. They were used strictly for heart surgery, the removal of the heart. The symbols on the sticks indicated in Mayan language that they held some mystical power when they were rubbed together on a heart that was removed from a sacrificial victim, of course no one volunteered to have his heart removed. The Mayans had these huge temples built in and around the Cancun area in Mexico. At the top of the temple was an altar just for heart removal or really sacrificial ceremony. The Mayans were not so nice, but they didn't mind it I guess. Anyway, our two sticks were determined to be ceremonial sticks that a priest held in each hand and after a heart was removed the priest would rub the sticks all over the heart and mutter religious sayings to the crowd of people down below the temple. The symbols on the two sticks indicated that the person who was sacrificed would go to the stars in the sky and live forever in paradise with a beautiful virgin. I have heard that before somewhere. I wonder how many hearts those two sticks actually touched. Joan said, coincidentally, that the price Terry and I accepted for the two sticks was exceptionally low. Historically, they were beyond value. I told Joan that I thought what we accepted in money was more than enough and I was glad that the University of North Dakota got them intead of Cornell University or anyone else. Terry agreed with what I said and he said "if we want more money, we will go and find more Indian aritifacts". We all laughed at that. However, it did plant a seed in my head. Maybe there are more artifacts out there and we missed them in our hurry to get out of those Black Hills with the two sticks we found. I said to Joan "maybe there are more artifacts out there, someone placed those two sticks there where we found them, and maybe there are more. I really never gave any thought about more until now, has anyone else thought about that"? Terry said while working one day he had a passing thought about more artifacts but never retained it. The girls said they were too busy working to give any thought to more items. So now I started something and once I get a thought process started it is very hard to let it go. I said to Terry and the girls "what if we spend a week in the Black Hills and see if we can find anything"? We agreed on a week that we all take off from work, a week's vacation together and go hunt artifacts. Terry and the girls looked at one another and thought about it and all smiled at once. Yes was the response, all at the same time. Lucy said "how about a honeymoon in the dirt? We spend our honeymoon searching for more artifacts where Bill & Terry found theirs". We could camp out and search and dig for a whole week. Boy I am glad I'm marrying an archaeologist. She likes to dig in dirt. 99% of women don't like to get their hands dirty, but I get one who does. Terry, Joan and I said, yes, that would be about as classical a honeymoon as there ever was. So, right then and there, we started planning our honeymoon.

We had a great week of visiting and doing things and then everyone had to get back to work. Terry took Joan home and went home himself. I took Lucy home and then flew back to Corning. Since I started at the airport, Walter has been like a father figure to me, always coming in to the shop and getting a cup of coffee and watching what I was doing. Sometimes he would suggest things about the plane I was working on, making it easy to solve some problem I had. It helped sometimes. We were close friends, I guess, we talked about many things while I worked or when I didn't have work. His wife, Martha, was a real sweetheart and many times after work or on the weekend when they knew I was alone, they would have me over for dinner. Sundays were the best, Martha could cook. During the winter, Walter, like me, had very little to do, so I would go over to his office and help him clean things up and help paint if he needed it done, odd things just to have something to do especially on the weekends. We got along great, of course I was working for food – Martha's cooking. They didn't have any children and I didn't ask why, so for some reason they took to me and I to them. Because of what Walter had done for me, I bought for them, on Christmas, a new car, not the best and not the cheapest either, but a nice new one. Walter was always driving around in an older model and it wasn't that reliable. Several times he had me look at it and though it was a minor repair, it had to be fixed. So, I thought that with all Walter had done for me by helping me get my pilot's license and letting me use a hangar along with, I am sure, work he got from other plane owners at the airport, a car was appropriate. Walter about had a fit and Martha said they couldn't accept a gift like that. I said "it's a done deal, you now have a new car to tool around in". Martha is a lot like Mom, a very affectionate woman and she threw her arms around my neck and gave me a hearty hug. She about squeezed me to death. Actually, subconsciously, I was securing more Sunday dinners by doing this. Walter could only express his happiness best by a hearty handshake and many, many thanks. That's all I wanted.

Spring was coming and work on the planes was doing good. All the owners wanted me to do a complete check up on their planes. Well not everyone, but I had more than enough work to do over the weekend and nights. Since work had pick up that much, I told my boss at the dealership that it was time to leave and I thanked him for allowing me to work there part time and for working with me. He said "the owner said whatever hours Bill wants to work, give him and when time comes for him to go back to the airport, let him go with much thanks on our part". These are good people I work for and greatly appreciated. So now I am back at the airport, now working and planning for June 1st.

With the distance between Terry and I, telephone is our only contact however, I want to get modern, so I went to an electronics store to see what I need for better communication with everyone. The salesman, which happened to be a young lady, asked if she could help me as I walked into the store. I said I was looking for some device to communicate with my brother in Rapid City, North Dakota, not just a telephone. She took me over to this section that had a bunch of tablets in it and explained all about them. I never had much time to ever explore all this new technology. I have been too busy working and learning and flying to notice a lot of this new stuff. However, she explained that what I needed was an iPad, a small-like computer used for many things, pictures, email, internet, lots of stuff. She said I could Skype my brother, and I said it is scalp not Skype and why I would want to scalp my brother. She laughed and said "Skype, not scalp. Skype is a form of video on the internet and you can talk to your brother and see him at the same time". I said "that's what I want. Sold, give it to me". She thought I was hilarious. Anyway, I bought it. I found out later that I could take pictures of planes that I was working on and keep, like a video library, a record of repairs. This way I had a record of all my repairs in case something happened and there was a plane crash. I didn't want any repercussions. I learned how to Skype Terry and it was more enjoyable to talk and see him. I did Skype Lucy, also. I love this modern technology.

Things have moved along nicely and before I knew it, June was here, really the end of May. I had all my repair work scheduled for after the honeymoon and all I needed to do for the wedding was show up. After the honeymoon, Lucy was going back to Minnesota to dig some more and I would return home. Terry and Joan had made plans to move into a new apartment somewhere near Joan's job at the university. Terry would commute to work. Of course, I had to get Lucy's and my camping gear ready along with our food supply for the week we were out in the desert. Terry would take care of his and Joan's gear. Mom & Dad thought we were nuts to spend a week on our honeymoon in the desert, but I told Mom that "that is what the girls like to do, it was their job, and a happy wife is a happy life". June 1ˢᵗ rolled around and the wedding took place in a small church near Mom and Dad's place. The girls didn't care which church we were married in or where. Lucy's parents were there, as were Joan's parents, Mom and Dad and a few friends, nothing elaborate. The girls were beautiful in their wedding dresses. Terry and I were lucky guys. Again, I thought about the two sticks and all that I had accomplished over the year since finding them. I still think of them as good luck charms. After the wedding and reception all four of us loaded up Terry's truck with our gear, along with two new four-wheelers and trailers that we rented, a trailer to carry them, and said goodbye to everyone and we departed for the Black Hills of North Dakota. We stayed overnight in a nice hotel and had a very nice dinner in their restaurant. The next day we arrived at our destination where Terry and I had started our 1ˢᵗ bike run. We unloaded the two four-wheelers and trailers, and loaded our supplies into the two trailers. Terry had made arrangements with a garage a ways back to keep his truck and trailer for the week. I followed Terry with one of the four-wheelers and picked him up and we went back to where the girls were. We picked up the girls and we headed off into the Black Hills. We found the spot where the two sticks were dug up and before we started digging, we set up camp, and made things comfortable for all of us. Lucy and I were about 20 feet away from Terry & Joan with a fire circle between. We brought as much firewood as we could, so we could have a fire a night. By the time we were all set up, it was getting late, so we called it a day.

The next morning we picked up our digging tools and we went looking back at the depression where Terry and I had slept a year ago. Joan surveyed the area, we showed her where the two sticks were and she said we should all start digging but be careful how we dig. We dug around that area all day and didn't find a thing. That evening after dinner we sat around the fire pit and talked about finding nothing. Joan said that perhaps the two sticks Terry and I found were place there in desperation and nothing else is around. I said "well, we have four more days to look". The next morning Terry and Joan went up the incline and Lucy and I went down. There was a little gulley that lead off to the west, so I said to Lucy "let's explore this gulley". I took out my knife and red marker tape and marked the entrance to that gulley. Then Lucy and I walked back into a narrow, but not too steep of a passage way. We went about 50 feet and the walls were getting narrower and darker back in there. I could see alright, but a flashlight would be helpful. Another thing we had to be careful of was snakes. This is June and it is warm out, and so are snakes. I told Lucy that we had better go back out and I would go get a flashlight before we continued deeper into the that gulley. She was ok with that. Lucy waited for me at the marker and I hightailed it up to camp. I got my flashlight and, with me holding Lucy's hand, we went deeper into the darkness. We went about another twenty feet, and the walls were so close Lucy had to walk behind me, when all at once I heard it. Damn, a rattler. I moved the light around and back by the wall was a pile of rags and there it was, laying on top of the rags daring us to come closer. Well, I know something about snakes and the last thing you want to be bitten by is a rattle snake. You can die before you get to the hospital, especially our here in the desert. Lucy was huffing and puffing and saying we have to get out of here. I said to her that the snake was just warning us to stay away from him. I looked at what he was laying on and thought what were rags doing way back here in this small gulley. I said to Lucy "look at that pile of rags, do you see anything"? And, I asked her what she thought rags were doing in here. She said she had no idea, but said "look over there to the right a little", and I moved the light over and there in the dirt was what looked like some kind of metal. I said "Lucy, let's get back out of here and go get Terry and Joan". She said "let's hurry out of here, I don't like snakes". I laughed but I knew that both of us didn't need Mr. Snake on us. We went back out of the gulley, went up the incline and found Terry and Joan digging. We asked if they had found anything yet. Both said no. I said "well hang on to your knickers kids because Lucy and I stumbled onto a find. I don't know what is there yet because Mr. Rattler wouldn't let me get close". Both of them asked a dozen questions, and I said "grab another flashlight and something to get rid of Mr. Snake and maybe some of his kids". All Lucy and I saw was one big one.

Lucy and I showed Terry and Joan where we were and Terry very nicely dispatched Mr. Snake. He was the only one in there, thank goodness. We arranged our lights so that we could see better. I had grabbed a lantern from my tent when I went to get Terry and Joan. Now we had plenty of light to see what was in that pile of rags. Before disturbing the rag pile, I had Terry look at that piece of metal I had seen. He moved over to it and picked it up gently. What he had in his hand was a sword, not very long, guessing maybe 2 feet, and it appeared to be somewhat rusty looking. Terry handed it to me, and

Joan and Lucy touched it and said "turn it over". I did. Joan was so excited and said this looked like a 14th century sword and the condition was remarkable for it's age. I said to Terry "go ahead and move the rags carefully because they may indicate someone's clothes". What looked like a pile of rags was an old ratty blanket that had deteriorated over the years. Terry slowly moved pieces of the blanket and with Joan beside him said "go slow". Terry and I are not archaeologists and we would probably just kicked that pile over to see what was there. But, thankfully, the girls were there to tell us how to move things around. Joan and Terry kept removing pieces of blanket very carefully and putting it into a pile. Pretty soon we could see more cloth but different than the blanket. It looked like some kind of uniform. Joan said "stop". Her and Terry did stop removing blanket material. I said to Joan "what do you see in there"? She said that this pile of clothes was a dead person. I said "you've got to be kidding", and Lucy said that it appeared to be some kind of a soldier and if it's age matched the sword, this could be a historical find, so that's why Joan said to stop. All this stuff in here needs to be documented. Well, our camera and notebooks were back at our camp, so Joan suggested that we go back and get what the girls needed to work this site. That's what Joan called it. It was lunch time anyway and everyone was getting hungry, so we backed out of the gulley and at the entrance I said to Joan "should I mark this wall here so we know where where to return to". She said no, that wasn't necessary, but I did take my knife out and carve into the sandstone wall an X like X marks the spot. Everyone laughed and Lucy said X is the treasure spot. We got back to camp and had some lunch.

Joan got out her camera and her note book and started writing in it. Her and Lucy were in a huddle, Terry and I sat around watching. The girls were in their element! Both of us smiled and Terry said "could we have found a better place to honeymoon than this"? I agreed with him. After a while, Joan said "we are ready to return to the gulley, but bring along some plastic bags, if we have any". I managed to find one large one that I had my shaving stuff in, so I dumped out my stuff and stuck the bag into my pocket. We went back down the incline to the gulley marked with my X, Joan snapping pictures all the way, Terry also brought another lantern, so we now had plenty of light back there. Joan handed the camera to Terry and said to take lots of pictures while we worked. Lucy got next to Joan and both girls knelt down next to the pile of clothes and started removing the remaining blanket to reveal what was there. I held one of the lanterns up so the girls had plenty of light to work with. As they removed more of the blanket, Terry and I heard ohs and ahs. When the blanket was totally removed, Joan said to stop. She needed to make notes in her book. The pile of clothes was something I had never seen. Joan finally said "I believe this is a conquistador, a Spanish soldier". We all digested that bit of information and after a bit I said "clear up here in North Dakota". I thought they were in the *southern, southwest part of* Arizona, New Mexico, area not up here. Joan said it is possible they got this far north but she would have to research that subject further, but as far as she could tell, that is what this pile is. So, her and Lucy again started removing, very slowly, cloth and then a bone appeared. It looked like part of the shoulder. Joan slowly removed it and asked for the plastic bag I had. She placed the bone in the bag along with some of the uniform from the pile. Then she said "we had enough for now,

I want to go home and back to the university to date this bone and cloth". She asked if we would mind because this happens to be really significant and extremely important, especially if it ties into the two sticks. Terry and I just looked at each other and I said "let's go". So, up the incline to camp we went, and it was getting late, so we decided that this would be the last night of our honeymoon. We would stay back in Grand Rapids the remaining time of our vacation. All agreed and the girls could work on our find. We decided to call the dig "the honeymoon project". That will get people talking. So we spent the last night talking about many things, getting to really know our mates. I don't know about Terry but things I learned about Lucy really made me happy, and a lot of things we like together. She was afraid of flying, but after going to Cornell last year, she said it wasn't bad. I said "wait 'til I take you up in my plane, you will appreciate flying a whole lot better". I told her that as soon as she could get away from her dig in Minnesota that I would like to take her home to visit her parents and to meet them. She said "that would be nice and she would let me know when she could leave the dig". The next morning we broke down camp and loaded up the trailers and headed out of the Black Hills to the garage where Terry left the truck and trailer. Before we left I had gone down to the gulley with the X on it and looked around. We had left a lot of foot prints, and if someone happened to stumble on this area they would see all if these footprints, so I took my jacket off and swung it back and forth on the path and wiped out footprints as I went up the incline. I did this for about 20 feet, now there was no indication anyone was there.

We arrived home at Mom and Dad's and they were surprised we were home early. Terry & I explained why we were home, but left out the discovery. We didn't need to let them in on what we found just yet. We just said we had had enough of roughing it in the desert. I told Mom & Dad that we would be leaving in the morning and going to the university, Joan and Lucy had something to take care of. Mom fed us while we were there and she got to know her daughters-in-law some more. Dad thought something was up but he said nothing, knowing us two boys. In the morning we kissed Mom and Dad goodbye and headed to Grand Rapids and the university. The night before, Joan had called Professor Dunham and said that they had found something of interest and would be in the next day for him to see.

We got to the university about 11:15 in the morning and went straight to Professor Dunham's office. He was waiting for us and we went into what was his lab. There was table, boxes, books, tools, you name it. To me it looked like a junk yard, but then again, if he was to come to my shop and look around, he would know he was in a junk yard. Joan placed the bag with the bones and cloth on the table. Professor Dunham looked it over and then looked at Joan and said "what do we have here"? Joan then began explaining what we did on our honeymoon, well not everything. She explained the pile of cloths in the gulley and pictures they took and what she thought was a conquistador. Professor Dunham was flabbergasted. He knew Joan and if she thought this might be a conquistador, then more than likely it was. So Joan said that to verify the "find" they need to date the cloth and get DNA samples from the bones and run a check for Spanish blood. He agreed and would send the sample to the necessary places. Joan then went to the computer and downloaded pictures from her camera into the computer. When completed, the picture showed everything we did the day before in the gulley, except me wiping out the footprints. Professor Dunham was in awe, he said "he would never believe that the conquistadors ever made it that far north". He said he would start researching right away. We left and went to lunch back at Lucy's diner and made plans for the next 2 days of our honeymoon. Terry and Joan said they wanted to look for an apartment in a location both could commute from, but not too far from either's work place. Lucy and I already talked about our future plans. She would be returning to Minnesota to dig and I would go home to work and when she could next get off, I would come and get her and we would go to Ohio to her parents home. I would miss my wife.

After lunch, Terry and I shook hands and I gave my sister-in-law a big hug and Terry did the same to Lucy. We said goodbye until we could get together again and I said "to call with the info whenever Joan found out, whatever it was we found". Lucy and I spent the next two days sightseeing around Grand Rapids, going to a movie, eating out and still getting to know each other. I found out her family settled in Ohio back in the 1800's and did crop farming now. She was the only child and also the first to graduate from college in her immediate family. Her Dad farmed 500 acres in a little town called Eaton and made a modest living from that, enough to send Lucy to college. They were happy that Lucy found someone to love and that would make her happy. She told her folks that, possibly, we could see them Thanksgiving. That's a ways off but Lucy has to dig until it gets too cold up there in Minnesota, so

Thanksgiving would be the soonest we would see them. Our time together came to an end and I put Lucy on a plane to Minnesota and I caught my plane to Corning.

Back home and at work lots of people congratulated me on my marriage and were glad I was home, especially Walter and Martha. I was happy also because Martha wanted me there at their house on Sunday for dinner, what's a guy to do? I loved these people. Summer had moved along pretty well. I kept in touch with my wife through the iPad. We Skyped and talked every few days in the evenings. I sure missed Lucy. She told me about her dig and what they were looking for up there in Minnesota. We had discussed her work many times before when we were together, so she keeps me informed every so often. It is rather interesting work, but slow going. It seems the University of North Dakota was looking at this particular area because it was believed or rumored that the Spanish had settled in that area a long, long time ago. After our two finds I am always interested in what Lucy says about her work.

On the 4th of July I was in my shop working on a plane's engine, which I had out of the plane and on a dolly – I was engrossed in my work that afternoon. I had the door open on the hanger to get some cool air in and around my work when I heard a sound like a bang and then screeching. I walked over to the door opening and looked out. I saw people yelling and pointing to the end of the airport, and, then, I saw a plane tail up in the air and smoking. About that time Walter drove up and yelled "a plane accident and get in". I ran around the truck and jumped in the front seat with Walter and he gunned the engine and took off in the direction of the accident. From the look of things as we approached the plane, there wouldn't be any survivors. We had fire extinguishers in the truck just for that purpose. When we got there I grabbed one and Walter grabbed another and as we approached the plane, there was a large explosion. The plane fuel tank had blown up. Both Walter and I threw ourselves down on the ground to avoid getting burnt and hit by flying debris. We both jumped up and started spraying foam as we approached the wreck. After a while we were accompanied by other people with fire extinguishers. We all sprayed foam on the wreck. We managed to knock down the flames enough to see the pilot, he was unconscious. I dropped my extinguisher and ran up to the side of the plane and grabbed ahold of the door handle and gave a hard yank on it. The door fell open and I reached in and unhooked his seatbelt and grabbed his jacket and hauled him out on to the tarmac. Others were there to assist me. We carried the pilot over to the edge of the runway and laid him on the grass. Among all the plane owners there are several EMT's and one happened to be at the airport that day and he was "Johnny on the spot". The pilot was an older man and I had done some work on his plane before, so I knew who he was. Apparently, he suffered a stroke just as he was coming in for a landing. The ambulance came and took him off to the hospital. Walter and everyone pounded me on the back for rushing in and getting the pilot out quickly. I just hope the poor guy lives, he looked pretty banged up laying there on the grass. Walter called for a wrecker to remove the plane. When he came, we helped load it and clean up the debris laying around, so no other plane would be damaged by anything laying around. We put the plane next to my hanger until the owner knew what he wanted to do about the damage, which was extensive. Personally, I would junk it myself. That was an exciting day. Worked went well and I managed to bank some money that summer.

Terry called around the middle of August and wanted to know if I could take a few days off of work and fly back to North Dakota. I asked him why and he said Joan and Dr. Dunham, again, had some news on the things we found back in June when we were on our honeymoon. I said I would reschedule my work so as I could take a week off and I would let him know just what date that would be. I talked with Walter and said I was taking a week off and I would get a stand-in mechanic that I had become friends with and he had helped me do several rebuilds when I was overloaded with work. He had come in when I called him and I like Karl a lot. He was very conscious of things as he worked on them. Walter knew Karl and knew I had used him at different times. I knew Karl could handle things while I was gone. Walter agreed. I went over my Piper Cub very carefully and did a ground check to make sure nothing was loose or worn. I checked everything over really good because I was going to fly to Grand Rapids with Cubby. I figured I could make it in 2 days, and not really push Cubby. I would have to stop for gas at different airports, but no problem, however I did plot my route and I filed a flight plan, which is required, but I knew how far I could go on a tank of gas and where an airport was. On the 24th, I packed a duffle bag for a week only. I also loaded up some groceries. I like to make sure I have food with me when I am off flying and especially a long flight. One never knows when you may need it. I called Terry and said I was flying out the third week of August and would be there probably on the 25th and I was flying Cubby. He wanted to know why I wasn't flying commercial and I said I wanted to fly home and while there, give Mom and Dad a day in the air. And, then I was going to fly to Minnesota to see Lucy, I missed my wife. Weather was supposed to be clear all the way into Illinois and by early afternoon I could get an update on the weather then. I took off with Cubby around 10:00 AM and took her up to 3,000 ft. and we just hummed along hour after hour. Toward late afternoon I checked my chart and saw I was coming into Illinois and my gas gauge was really low. I called ahead to an airport on my chart, called for a landing and gas, I was cleared to come in and directed to the gas pump. After filling Cubby up and checking the oil, I pulled over and parked out of the way, I locked Cubby up and went into the office to pay for my gas and the closest restaurant directions. There was a restaurant at the end of the building and I could walk there. While in the office I got the weather report for flying further to the west, and asked if I was ok for tie down where I was. They said I was in a good spot. I do not like to leave Cubby without tying her down. I never trust the weather overnight. Anyway, I ate supper and found a motel not far from the airport. I got a good night's sleep and was ready to fly again the next morning. I got into Grand Rapids late into the afternoon on the 25th. After taking care of Cubby I rented a car at the airport, called Terry to let him know I was there, and I was staying in a hotel and I would see him tomorrow. It was a long flight, but I like to fly.

I called Lucy from the hotel and told her I was in Grand Rapids and I would see her in Minnesota, soon, after I met with Terry, Joan and Professor Dunham. Lucy already knew about me coming to the meeting. Joan has kept Lucy informed on what was going on with our honeymoon "find". Of course, I talked to my wife almost every day since we parted. I did miss her. I met up with Terry the next day at Professor Dunham's office. Terry and Joan were already in the office when I got there. Professor Dunham called us into his office and all the stuff we found was laying out on the table really neat. We shook hands with Professor Dunham and then he started. He explained that the cloths we found in that pile under the blanket were very old. He had carbon dated the clothes, pieces of blanket and the bones, and that the cloth was dated about 1350. He was surprised that any of it survived to this day, but because of the arid climate in the Black Hills and the location of the find, everything was somehow preserved. After he dated the clothes, he did DNA on the bones and was not too surprised to learn that they revealed a person with Spanish blood. Further investigation also revealed that these bones belonged to a Conquistador who was in the Spanish army and an invasion force lead by a General Alveraze, a small army of about 200 men, donkeys and equipment. What they were doing this far north no one knows, and no one knows what happened to General Alveraze and his army. There is no known Spanish invasion army that ever made it this far into North America, and what this particular soldier was doing in the Black Hills no one will ever know. And, what was his connection to the two sticks we found earlier, and did he even know about them because they were found about 20-30 feet up hill from where he was found. The question I had was were the sticks buried by some other soldier as they climbed up out of that area where we found the sticks and the Conquistador, and how many were in General Alveraze's army or was there just a few men left. One could only speculate on what happened.

The sword was also interesting Professor Dunham said. The condition was poor but valuable being what it was, so Professor Dunham got right down to the nuts and bolts of the situation and said that what we found was exceptional and very rare and that the university was interested in purchasing our find and was prepared to pay $100,000 dollars for the Conquistador. Joan knew about the money offer, but Terry, Lucy and I didn't, and when Professor Dunham made that announcement, we just stood there and stared at him for about two minutes and then the shock wore off. I looked at Terry and he looked at me and said if it was ok with the girls and Bill, we would accept that offer. I said yes and the girls said yes, after all, they had a right to express their opinion. I had Lucy on the iPad, so she was also present, but in Minnesota. We shook hands on the sale with Professor Dunham and he said he could cut us a check however we wanted it done. I said to Terry how about 2 checks, one for you and Joan and one for Lucy and I? He agreed and Professor Dunham said if you wait I will do that now and you folks can have your money before you leave. We said ok. I said to Terry and Joan "that that was a prosperous honeymoon", and I said to Lucy on the iPad that we can go now on another honeymoon wherever she wanted to go. We all laughed at that. Lucy said she had to get back to work and I said I would see her tomorrow in Minnesota. She said to be careful flying up. We got our checks and I hugged both Terry and Joan and said I had to get to Mom and Dad's and that I wanted to take them for a spin in Cubby. We said our goodbyes and I left for the airport.

I flew into Rapid City and rented another car and drove to Mom & Dad's place. The trouble was it was getting late and Mom had dinner on when I got there, so I waited until the next morning to take them up in Cubby. Mom wasn't too much for the idea, but Dad convinced her that everything was ok! So the next morning we went to the airport and I did my thing getting Cubby ready while Mom and Dad waited by the plane. I finished my visual check and loaded up the folks into the plane. 3 people in Cubby is tight, but we did it. We took off and Mom started squealing and saying "I'm scare, I'm scared". Both Dad and I calmed her down and after a while she relaxed and we cruised about 3,000 ft. I took them for an hour ride. Mom loved it, Dad was happy as a lark. He had never flown in a small plane before. I landed and took them home, had lunch, hugged and kissed both of them and left for Minnesota. I wanted to be with Lucy as much as I could for the next day or two. anyway, I made it to Minnesota late in the day and after securing Cubby, I rented a car and met my wife at her apartment. She was waiting for me all worried that something had happened to me. Lucy got the next day off and we did several things together, and spent the time talking and still getting to know each other. We really didn't have much time together other than the honeymoon. We discussed what we wanted to do with our share of the money we had gotten, and both agreed to bank it for a house in the future. $50,000 would make a nice down payment on a house. Before I knew it, two days was over and Lucy went back to her dig and Cubby and I took off for Corning. I pretty much followed the route I took going to Grand Rapids. I returned home with no problems. Cubby and I had a nice trip. I returned to work and found Karl had everything under control. I talked to Walter and he told me that the pilot that crashed his plane earlier was alive and well, but he won't be flying again. It seems as though he suffered severe internal injuries and doctors told him no more flying. I imagine that didn't sit too well with him. His plane was to be trashed because of the condition it was in. Karl said the insurance guy came to look it over and said it was a total loss. So, he said to Karl that if we wanted it for storage fees, it was ours. He accepted it for me knowing I could use things off of it in my repairs. The motor was sound, no damage and a few other things were good. I talked to Karl about the amount of work I had to do. It seems that the word of mouth got around and other plane owners wanted my service and it was getting to the point that I had more than I could handle and I was falling behind. Karl, through conversation with him, wasn't happy where he was working, some small shop in Corning, so I said to him a few days after my trip "Karl, I need help in this shop because I'm falling behind in the work load and you see how it is". I said to Karl "why don't you come to work for me full time. You know me and the shop and pretty much everything about these small planes we work on. I need a good mechanic and you are one". He laughed at my way of saying things. I would hire him if he said yes, well he did. Karl turned in his notice and two weeks later he came to work for me. Now I was an employer, so I called Terry for advice on tax matters and such. Now I had to make room for Karl in the hanger for his work space. We both fixed up a work bench for him and a place for his tool box. Walter helped some, but I think he drank more coffee than he worked.

Last winter I went back to the dealership where I used to work, but this winter coming up I will keep working in the hanger with my employee, so I have to make accommodations for keeping warm while working. I called in a contractor to make a work place warm enough to work in. I ran all this through Walter because, so far, Walter hasn't charged me for rent and I respect his advice. He said I was ok and with this amount of planes in the airport increasing every season, I could keep doing what I am doing. It's true that there was an increase of planes and pilots over the last two years because more work came in to the shop, and that's why I needed additional help. The contractor set up part of the hangar towards the back wall with enough room for one plane and hung up long plastic strips that were moveable, and added a good heating system overhead. Now we could work and be comfortable doing it in the winter, and if it gets to cold, we will close up for a while. I got a call from Lucy about the middle of September wanting me to come to Minnesota and could I take some time off? I said I could fly up and stay for maybe several days and that Karl could handle things while I was gone. So, I prepped Cubby and at the end of September, I took off for Minnesota. It took me two days of flying to get there. I landed at a small airport 10 miles from where Lucy worked and lived. The owner and I talked for some time after I landed, nosey kind of guy, but friendly. I told him about Corning and my work and where I was going. He didn't know much about where Lucy worked, but he was interested in my job and what I did. He said good airplane mechanics were hard to find and wondered if I was looking for work. He had several mechanical jobs that needed help real bad. I told him I wanted to spend time with my wife, and didn't really have time for anything else. I asked him what it was that he needed done and he said one plane needed a new propeller and tune-up. Another had electrical problems that no one seemed to be able to fix and the plane owners were getting rather testy about not being able to use their planes It didn't sound like either job was that big and I told him that when I came back to go home I would take a look at both planes. I asked him where I could rent a car for a few days and he said I would have to go into town to do that and that was about 10 miles, but he said "why don't you take my car, I don't need it for a while. I don't go anywhere"? I thought "wow" this guy doesn't know me, but is willing to lend me his car. I shook his hand and introduced myself and he said his name was Bryan and he was the owner of this small airport. I thanked Bryan for the use of his car and I got his phone number in case I was late. I met up with Lucy at her apartment later that day and after cleaning up I took her out to dinner. We went to a nice restaurant. We had dinner and a bottle of wine and we talked and talked, and talked. I told her about Bryan and the 2 jobs he had and the car he loaned me. She said "he must be some nice guy to loan you his car". I said "I thought so"! Lucy then told me why she wanted me to come up to Minnesota. It seems that her head of the dig, a Professor Whittley, wanted to talk to me about our discoveries. Lucy had mentioned our finds to him. Of course he knew Professor Dunham at the University of North Dakota. I think all of these professors know each other or about each other, especially in their own profession. Anyway, Lucy said Professor Whittley was interested in discussing our finds. She had made an appointment with him for the next day at the "dig". This would be my first encounter at an archaeological dig. The next day we met Professor Whittley out in this field. There were tents set up all over the place. People were digging in holes and others were sifting dirt the first bunch dug up. I used to play in dirt, but these people get paid to play in dirt. Professor Whittley and I shook hands and he asked me if I knew what was going on here? I only knew what Lucy had told me and that was very little. He explained that somewhere around the 14th century, about 1350 AD, Spanish Conquistadors under a General Alveraze, marched north and east to this area, perhaps trying to find his way to the Great Lakes and maybe home, but the weather had done him in. His small army got here as winter set in and from Professor Whittley's research, weather, then, was terrible and he thinks that they got either snowed in or froze to death. They have uncovered bones of soldiers and a few donkeys, maybe deer and small game. His opinion is that they got snowed in and starved to death or froze. I asked him how he knew it was General Alveraze. "Through research of Spanish documents and Indian folklore". He said "maybe the Indians did Alverize in, we haven't really looked in that direction yet". We also found buttons, swords, utensils, all indicating General Alveraze was here. DNA was performed and it is confirmed that the bones are of Spanish extraction. So, we are 95% sure this site is the end of General Alveraze. I then said that the Conquistador we found in the Black Hills was Spanish, but what connection did the two sticks have to do with him? Professor Whittley said "I doubt that the two sticks, which appear to be Indian, had anything to do with the soldier you found. I have discussed this with Professor Dunham in North Dakota and we come to the same conclusion, what the two medicine sticks you found by themselves mean, we don't know. By that I mean, what if anything, the two sticks were left by some Medicine Man, or maybe they were looted from Mexico, we just don't know". From talking to Professor Whittley, the poor fellow our group found in the Black Hills was more than likely from this group here in Minnesota. We all agreed to that fact. Our poor soldier might have been sick and died or the Indians got him, although we didn't find any Indian items with our soldier. Very likely he was sick and they left him behind. Another prospective is he might have gotten lost and ended up there all by himself. Who knows what happened to the poor fellow, but still in all, our sticks still stick out by themselves, and questions about their content and location are still a mystery. Professor Dunham has been working with the Mexican archaeologist from Cancun, Mexico, and that's where the Aztec Indians once lived. So, we wait and see what he comes up with. I had a good day with Professor Whittley, but I wanted to get my wife alone because time was moving on.

I spent the rest of the day rest of the day and the next day with Lucy. I didn't want to leave her but she had work and I needed to get home for my work. I didn't like leaving Karl alone too long, even though he could handle everything, I just want to know what's going on. I drove back out to the airport and gave Bryan back his keys and thanked him with a full tank of gas. I asked Bryan about those two jobs he wanted me to look at. He took me into the back of this hanger where both planes sat. The plane with the propeller problem didn't take more than 2 hours to change out with Bryan's help, but the plane with the electrical problem took me well into the evening and I finally found it. The plane has to have an electrical ground and the ground wire had come loose from it's mounting. It wasn't totally loose, but enough to cause the plane not to start and if it did, any movement or bumps, the electrical connection would break and the motor would quit and no lights. Bad situation if you are flying and you hit heavy winds which buffer planes all over, well you know what would happen, not good. Anyway, Bryan was happy that I fixed the two planes. He said "the owners would be happy to get their planes back" and then he said "why don't you come home with me and have supper with me and the wife, and stay the night and you can be off in the morning"? I had not planned on anything that evening and definitely didn't have a place to stay. Sometimes I sleep in "Cubby" when other accommodations are not available. So I said "I would be happy to stay over the night with him and his wife". "Good he said, I'll call the missus and let her know we are on our way home". I spent the night with Bryan and his wife and the next morning, we went back to the airport and I got Cubby ready for our trip home. I checked everything out and filled her gas tank which took 45 gallons of gas which would give me about 4 hours or more of flying time. I went to pay my bill with Bryan and he said "no charge". He said that what I did for him we were square with each other. I hadn't even thought of charging him to repair those two planes and we argued for a while but Bryan insisted I owed him nothing. I thanked him several times and fired up Cubby and left Minnesota. I got home the day after and was somewhat tired from all that flying. I got in late that day and Karl had already left for home while Walter knew I was coming. He waited for me to come down and land and as soon as I got Cubby secured we went home to his place and Martha. I told them everything that happened that week. Walter said more planes were showing up and, of course, more work for me. Walter said he was going to expand the airport and put in more hangers. It would be a large expense but with business picking up, he needed to accommodate these guys and their planes. He said next spring he would start. Now it is too late and cold weather is coming.

Another winter in New York. Flying time is about over for most pilots and they want their planes checked over and put away in their hangers for the winter. Karl and I provided that service, all a plane owner has to do is call and tell us to put such and such plane in storage and we do several things to put planes to sleep as I call it. The owners are happy for the service, they don't have to do anything, and in the spring they call and tell us they want their plane out of the hanger and prepped for flight. We do that. Service with a smile and I need a truck to haul my money to the bank. I provide a service and I get paid for it. For the most part, Karl and I had repair work most of the winter. On really cold days when trying to heat a large area, it doesn't pay, so we don't work on planes then. Karl has a part time job doing car and truck repairs, enough to keep him in money. I go home to Grand Rapids and my wife.

During the winter Lucy works on stuff from her dig and I see Professor Dunham now and then. Of course, Lucy and I visit Terry and Joan on the weekends. Terry says that from all he could tell with the info I was sending him, my business was going very well. He said to keep it up. He said I had a very profitable year, even paying an employee. I told him about Walter expanding the airport and all the new business it would bring. I had been thinking about another employee to help handle the work load, especially if the airport expands. Terry and Joan said they would be looking to buy a house next spring, and with their share of the money they could afford to buy a rather nice house. I didn't say anything, but I think I'm going to be an Uncle sometime soon. Lucy and I put having kids on hold for some time because of her work and my work distance. We have a strained marriage but we are working on it. Distance doesn't help when two people are apart. I love Lucy and I really want this marriage to work, and I think Lucy does also. We will see how it goes over the next year. Mom and Dad feel bad about it and offer advice, but things are what they are. I also try to spend time with Mom and Dad during the winter when I have more time to do so. I help Dad repair things around the house and work on their car. Mom is so happy that I come home often. She loves Lucy. Lucy and Joan are like daughters she never had.

Christmas came up soon enough and for me and Lucy, this being our 1st anniversary, I thought I would take her to Hawaii. She was thrilled about the idea. Terry and Joan came home to Mom and Dad's and we all celebrated our 1st anniversary. Terry and Joan confirmed what I thought about me being an Uncle. Joan was up and expecting sometime in June. Mom and Dad about exploded when Joan told them the news. They were going to be Grandparents. We all congratulated Terry and Joan. That's why they were looking for a home to purchase. Apartments are no place to raise children. Lucy and I did go to Hawaii for a week and everything seemed ok. Lucy and I were very close, but I felt that sometimes Lucy was holding back things. But, we did have a nice week in Hawaii.

Lucy had to return to North Dakota University to work on her Bachlor degree and therefore I returned home to Corning. I spent a few days with Mom and Dad and then I left for Corning. On days that weren't all that cold I went to work in the hanger and Karl would show up occasionally and Walter hung around most of the time. I think he was bored staying in his office.

There wasn't all that much he had to do in the winter but answer the phone. I spent a lot of time at Walter's home because I had nowhere else to go and also Martha's cooking was better than mine. I don't know if I said it before but both Walter and Martha were good friends and I felt that they were more like a mother and father to me. Spring finally came around and business picked up. Karl was back working full time as we had to prep our customers' planes for summer use. We had more work than we could handle but we managed to handle everything. I think we serviced around 25 planes in the month of April, nothing major, mainly change oils, grease what was needed, fuel the planes up, general servicing is what we did, and the pilots were happy that we did all that. They didn't have to do it and they paid well for our service.

Lucy finished another year at school and they want her back up in Minnesota, again, to continue with the dig she had previously worked on. We talked off and on over the winter, and she sounded a little off on conversations, but I figured she was tired from school work and then going back to work right after school with no time off. To me, I thought she needed a rest, but she said no. I let her know my work was getting real heavy and getting time away would be hard this summer, but that I really missed her. She sounded distant to me. Sometime in late May, I met this plane owner from a small town north of Corning and he needed a major overhaul on his Cessna. Apparently he wasn't careful with the maintenance of his aircraft and the engine was in need of an overhaul. He wanted me to do it, but his finances were not the best and he proposed a trade. I had given him an estimate for the work and he almost fainted, but plane engines are very expensive however, that plane that crashed last year was still sitting outside my hanger and I knew the engine was good in it, and would easily sit in his aircraft. So, I knew where I stood with cost to get him back up in the air. He said he had a small farm that he wasn't all that interested in and wondered if I was interested enough to make a trade. I was and I wasn't if you know what I mean, so I told him I would consider it, but I needed to see the property. We agreed to go the next day and he would pick me up at the airport around 9:00 am. Well, this is the first time I considered being a home owner. I know I talked to Lucy about buying a home someday with our $50,000 from the find, but never thought now and also a farm. At 9:00 am this guy shows up and off we go to his place that he wants to trade for work. We probably went about 12 miles out of Corning and went up this valley and the sun was just coming over the hill. What a beautiful valley. We drove almost to the end of the valley where the hill was, and I am thinking a big hill, perhaps 1500 feet high. The sun was just coming onto the land at 9:30 in the morning. We stopped at this place and he said it is small but a pretty nice place, so I got out and looked things over. It was a small rance house on about 4 acres, and had a small creek running behind it, nice flat ground. The house looked ok, so I said I would like to see the inside. He unlocked the door and we went in. I looked everything over and came to the conclusion that this guy must be nuts. The value for this place is far and above what work I would do on his plane. I confronted him on this and he said "I am getting a divorce and I don't want my wife to get any more than what she has already gotten out of me. You fix my plane so I can fly out of Corning and you can have this place". I thought, holy smokes, this is a great deal so I shook his hand and said "then it's a deal". He got all the paperwork on the farm prepared and all I had to do was sign. I finished fixing up his plane and he was happy that everything went well and quickly, because he wanted out of Corning before his wife and her lawyer could catch up with him. He flew off and I had myself a small farm worth far more than the work I put into his plane. He was happy that his wife wasn't getting the farm or his plane, he was gone! Walter said that what he did was the craziest thing ever. Karl couldn't believe that people do things like that. I called Terry and told him what I did and he laughed about it saying "you sure fell into a good thing". I said "maybe the sticks still work" and he said" they were". I called Lucy one evening and told her what transpired and she didn't seem so happy about it. She said she didn't like farm life and smelly animals, even though there weren't any animals on the place. Her attitude surprised me, but I let it go. I was now a property owner and I moved in after a week of cleaning up the place and boy did I like it, not far from work and a very nice home. I didn't tell Lucy the whole story about how I got the farm. The part about him divorcing his wife, I didn't feel she needed to know. I just told her I was offered this farm for practically nothing and bought it with my money from work. She wasn't exactly happy with what I did because we were suppose to look for a place together, but I look at it this way, when a deal presents itself and a person doesn't take advantage of it, they lose. So anyway, I have a nice little farm. Lucy and I talked about going to Ohio to see her parents, and again, Thanksgiving week would be as soon as I could leave work, and Lucy's dig would be closed up for the winter. So, we made plans to meet at the airport in Akron on November 25th as close to 3:00 pm as possible and we would drive to her parents place in Eaton. That was our plans for Thanksgiving.

Things at the airport were getting hectic and I had more work than Karl and I could handle, and I didn't want to hire more help. Overseeing one person was enough. I am not the boss type. With Karl, it is more like he's a partner, always working when needed and no complaints, just an easy going guy. So, as work kept coming in and was more than I could handle, I had to turn it down which wasn't popular, but as I explained it to the plane owners, I didn't want to get in over my head with work and then become sloppy and rushed in finishing a job, and cause a plane owner injury or death from my failure to provide the best work I could. When I put it that way I didn't get any grief. Perhaps I should maybe put the business up for sale. When I started this job at the airport I didn't think that I would have this much business, but once plane owners saw that I provide a good service, most everyone at the airport wanted me to service their planes. I would have to give the idea more thought. I figured I would run it by Walter and Martha and get their opinion. After all, Walter got me into this repair business.

June came and went, no baby yet for Terry and Joan, however, Terry said on the phone the other day that Joan should deliver by the 4th of July or the doctor will take it. The 4th is on a weekend and work still needed to be done. I had nothing that was pressing, so I gave Karl the week off and I headed for North Dakota and Lucy. Lucy was able to extend her 4th of July day off by one more day, so we had two days to spend together. She seemed excited when I arrived at her apartment but buy the end of two days I knew things weren't good with us, but I didn't say anything thinking things will be better in the future, a guy thing! So, I still had 3 days left and I went to see my nephew, which came on the 4th like the doctors said. Terry was the proud pa-pa when he showed me his son. I was very happy for Terry and Joan and thought someday I will have a son. I also went home to see Mom and Dad for a fe w days and tended to any problems they might have. Mom was so happy to be a Grandma that she couldn't keep quiet. The whole time I was there, she wanted to know what was the matter with me, "Terry produced a beautiful son, what about you"? I told Mom time would tell and Lucy and I wanted to wait for the right time. We weren't ready yet to have children. I didn't let on that things with Lucy and myself was not looking so good. It would hurt enough for Mom if things didn't work out with Lucy and I. I was beginning to have my doubts as to where this marriage of mine was heading. I suppose that distance didn't help any, when you see your wife for only a few days a year. The marriage can and has been strained. I never gave it any thought. I figured that with both working and we did have a goal, that distance wouldn't matter, but apparently it has. I don't know if she has a new interest or not but she does work with a lot of men and students on her dig. I went back to Corning and work with doubt on my mind.

Towards the end of August, I had supper at Walter's house. After we ate I brought up the subject of selling the repair business and that it was getting to be a job for me instead of pleasure. After explaining to them my reasons, Walter agreed that there was too much work for two men to handle and suggested expanding the work space and hiring more men. I agreed that that could be done but I didn't want to be an employer for a bunch of men. Karl was different, he was a good man and a friend, but hiring more men was not what I wanted to do, or supervise and the cost to add on to the hanger, to me it wasn't worth it. Walter and Martha agreed that it was getting to be too much for two men and said "whatever you decide is ok with us, though we hate to see you leave. You have made a huge success out of just one hanger and one extra man. Pilots will miss your work. Maybe Karl would keep the repair service going. Have you given any thought as to him taking over?" I had thought at one time that maybe he would be interested in the business if I decided to move away. I never mentioned it to Karl, but maybe I should. A few weeks later when work was piling up I said to Karl "would you like to continue our repair service and business on your own"? I then told Karl I was thinking of selling out and I wanted him to have first choice and I would establish a price and let him make payments. Karl, of course, jumped at the suggestion and said "he would love to have the chance to take over". So, I made the arrangements to sell everything to Karl and would stay until we close up in November.

Then the bomb hit, we were finishing up storage service for the few remaining planes the first week of November and it was cold out. Really we should have been done by the 1st of November, but weren't. Lucy called me in the middle of the day, which she hardly ever did. She sounded very cool and said "I want a divorce". When I asked why she said "that our marriage was a sham. We never see each other, we were miles apart and she was lonely and found someone else to keep her company". Really, I don't blame her, but I thought we had a plan, however plans don't always work out, I guess. I pleaded with her and said I would come to North Dakot and we could work things out. "No" she said. 'I am done with you and our marriage. The divorce papers are on the way. Please sign them and return the papers to my lawyer as soon as possible". Then Lucy hung up. I felt like a truck hit me. I know things weren't good but not that bad. If that was the way she wanted it, then I won't fight it. I love Lucy but it wasn't meant to be. We had too many things against us to start with.

Christmas I spent with Mom & Dad and, of course, they had to know about Lucy. Mom & Dad were sad that we broke up, and I also told them I sold the flying business. I saw Terry and Joan and my nephew. Boy he was getting big. Terry asked what happened with Lucy, but I am sure he already heard it from Joan with her and Lucy being close friends and all I could say was "it didn't work out". Both Terry and Joan said they were sorry for us and had hoped the marriage would have worked out. With that said, I told them I wished Lucy luck and I would move on. Terry asked what my plans were now that I wasn't married and had sold my business. I told him I wasn't sure and I was heading home to my place in New York for the winter.

Arriving home, I found that I didn't have anything to do sense I had sold the business to karl. I did go in on occasions to visit and help him on a few things, and visit with Walter and Martha, of course I stayed for dinners. But mostly I stayed at the farm, I had a lot of work I wanted do fixing up the place, so I stayed relatively busy. Spring came around and thing's got pretty busy around the place, cleaning up winter storm messes, fixing a multitude of things that the previous owner failed to fix, which I figured he didn't care about anyway with his marriage crapping the bed. And I had neighbors across the street that I had met during the winter and we talked on occasions. Then things Happened and I guess that the luck I had with the sticks was leaving me behind. Loosing Lucy was one and this mess that was now hitting Ny. On May 29,of 2008 See my next book out called Earth and The Aftermath. As the Title indicated this is "ABSOLUTELY an intriguing story" was it not !!

Printed in the United States
By Bookmasters